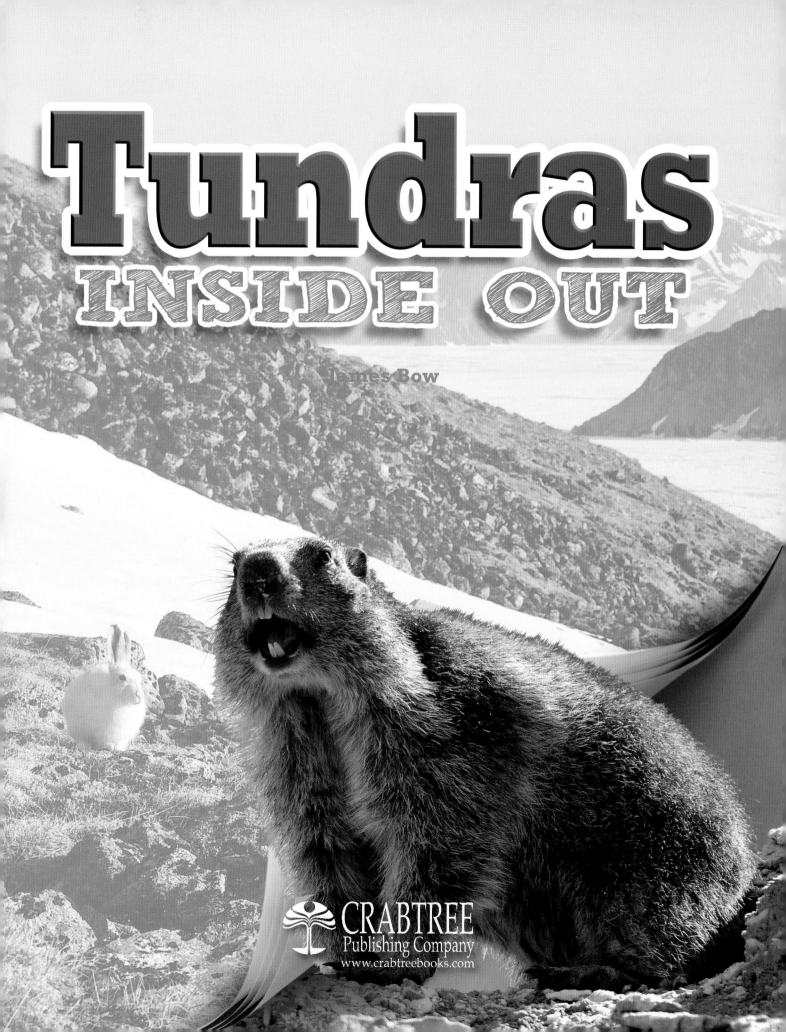

Tundras
INSIDE OUT

James Bow

CRABTREE
Publishing Company
www.crabtreebooks.com

Ecosystems INSIDE OUT

Author: James Bow
**Publishing plan research
    and series development:** Reagan Miller
Editorial director: Kathy Middleton
Editors: Sarah Eason, Jennifer Sanderson,
    Nancy Dickmann, and Shirley Duke
Proofreader: Wendy Scavuzzo
Project coordinator: Sarah Eason
Design: Paul Myerscough
Photo research: Rachel Blount
**Production coordinator and
    Prepress technician:** Tammy McGarr
Print coordinator: Katherine Berti

Written, developed, and produced by Calcium

Photo Credits:

t=Top, bl=Bottom Left, br=Bottom Right

Dreamstime: Volkan Akgul: p. 13 (tr); Andreanita: p. 21 (br); Galyna Andrushko: p. 12–13; Sharon Day: p. 19 (br); Aleksandr Frolov: p. 14–15; Paul Loewen: p. 4–5; Mihailzhukov: p. 15 (br); Naturablichter: p. 23 (br); Stephan Pietzko: p. 8–9, p. 18–19; Premekm: p. 16–17; Alexander Sidyakov: p. 11 (br), 28–29. FLPA: Pierre Vernay/Biosphoto: p. 1, p. 22–23. NASA: Michael Studinger: p. 10–11. Science Photo Library: Penn State University: p. 25 (tr). Shutterstock: Chbaum: p. 3; Maksym Deliyergiyev: p. 6–7; Incredible Arctic: p. 17 (br); Jeannette Katzir Photog: p. 9 (br); Yongyut Kumsri: p. 24–25; Christian Musat: p. 1. Wikimedia Commons: Ansgar Walk: p. 26–27; Flying Puffin: p. 27 (tr); Twiddleblat: p. 20–21.

Cover: Dreamstime: Erectus; Tom Linster (br).

Library and Archives Canada Cataloguing in Publication

Bow, James, 1972-, author
       Tundras inside out / James Bow.

(Ecosystems inside out)
Includes index.
Issued in print and electronic formats.
ISBN 978-0-7787-0639-7 (bound).--
ISBN 978-0-7787-0724-0 (html).--
ISBN 978-1-4271-7650-9 (pdf).--ISBN 978-1-4271-7644-8 (html)

       1. Tundra ecology--Juvenile literature. 2. Tundra animals-
-Juvenile literature. I. Title.

QH541.5.T8B68 2014   j577.5'86   C2014-903618-3
                                                                       C2014-903619-1

Library of Congress Cataloging-in-Publication Data

Bow, James.
 Tundras inside out / James Bow.
       pages cm. -- (Ecosystems inside out)
 Includes index.
 ISBN 978-0-7787-0639-7 (reinforced library binding) --
ISBN 978-0-7787-0724-0 (pbk.) --
ISBN 978-1-4271-7650-9 (electronic pdf) --
ISBN 978-1-4271-7644-8 (electronic html)
1. Tundra ecology--Juvenile literature. 2. Tundras--
Juvenile literature. I. Title.

 QH541.5.T8B68 2015
 577.5'86--dc23

                                          2014020249

Crabtree Publishing Company
www.crabtreebooks.com   1-800-387-7650

Printed in Hong Kong/082014/BK20140613

**Published in Canada
Crabtree Publishing**
616 Welland Ave.
St. Catharines, Ontario
L2M 5V6

**Published in the United States
Crabtree Publishing**
PMB 59051
350 Fifth Avenue, 59th Floor
New York, New York 10118

**Published in the United Kingdom
Crabtree Publishing**
Maritime House
Basin Road North, Hove
BN41 1WR

**Published in Australia
Crabtree Publishing**
3 Charles Street
Coburg North
VIC, 3058

Contents

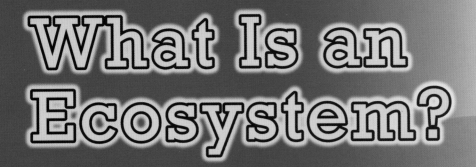

What Is an Ecosystem?

Plants and animals depend on many things to survive. They need sunshine, water, air, soil, and a temperature that is neither too hot nor too cold. These nonliving things are called **abiotic factors**. Plants and animals also need one another to survive. These living things are **biotic factors**. An **ecosystem** is made up of **organisms**, the environment in which they live, and their **interrelationships**.

How Big Are Ecosystems?

An ecosystem can be as small as a rock, or it can stretch for thousands of miles (kilometers). A **biome** is a large geographical area containing a number of similar plants, animals, and environments. Tundras, rain forests, grasslands, oceans, and deserts are biomes.

What Is Tundra?

The closer an area is to Earth's poles, the colder it becomes, and the harder it is for trees to survive. Eventually, it becomes so cold that no trees can grow because there is no fresh water. The tundra **climate** is cold and dry, with long winters and cool summers. The permanently frozen layer of ground that never thaws also prevents tree roots from growing deep into it. This point is called a tree line. The ecosystems beyond this tree line are called tundra. Tundra is a Russian word meaning "treeless mountain tract."

Let's explore tundra ecosystems around the world. We'll take a look at each ecosystem as a whole, then zoom in on one specific part of it.

What Is a System?

A **system** is a group of separate parts that work together for a purpose. An ecosystem helps ensure the survival of its living parts. Sunshine, water, soil, plants, insects, and animals are some of the parts of an ecosystem. Each abiotic and biotic factor has a specific and important role to play that helps the ecosystem function.

Organisms in an ecosystem are **interdependent**. If one part of an ecosystem fails or changes, other parts are affected, too.

Key

- Deserts
- Grasslands
- Oceans
- Rain forests
- Tundras
- Wetlands

This map shows where tundras and other biomes are found around the world.

Many tundra plants grow and **bloom**, or flower, in the summer. At other times of year, animals such as musk oxen must survive by eating food such as sparse grasses and shrubs. They travel for miles (kilometers) in search of food.

Energy in Ecosystems

Organisms cannot live without energy. Energy comes from the sun and is spread across the ecosystem through food. Organisms need one another for energy. This is known as a food chain.

The Energy Chain

Every food chain includes three main types of organisms. Plants are the main producers. They make their own food through a process called **photosynthesis**.

Next in the chain are consumers. Animals are consumers. They get their energy by eating plants, or eating animals that eat plants. Herbivores eat plants. Carnivores are meat-eaters. Some carnivores eat herbivores, and others eat carnivores. Omnivores eat both plants and animals.

The last part of the chain is the decomposers. These organisms, such as **fungi** and **bacteria**, eat dead plants and animals. They break them down and return **nutrients** to the soil. Plants take in the nutrients, and the food chain begins again.

A Food Network

Every living thing is connected in many ways to other living things, so a better term for the flow of energy between the many organisms is a **food web**. When two or more food chains overlap, they form a food web. A healthy food web has many different **species** of plants and animals. This is called **biodiversity**. A healthy food web also has many abiotic factors in the form of sunshine, good quality soil, and a lot of water.

lichens

caribou

Arctic wolf

This food chain shows the flow of energy from one organism to another.

Lichens come in many colors. They are often silver-gray or green, but they can also be red, yellow, or orange.

Eco Up Close

Lichens are made up of two organisms that work together in a **symbiotic relationship**, called mutualism, that is beneficial or helpful to both organisms. Lichens are made up of an **algae** with **chlorophyll** and a fungus, which provides minerals and nutrients to the algae. The chlorophyll allows the algae to make food, which helps feed the fungus. In turn, the fungus protects the algae from the wind and the environment. The fungus grows into a structure that clings to the rocky ground inside which the more delicate algae can live. Lichens are at the bottom of the tundra ecosystem. Without them, herbivores would have nothing to eat. Lichens also break up rocks. By doing so, it makes the first pieces of soil, which allows other plants to take root.

7

Northern Canada

In northern Canada treeless **plains** cover part of the Northwest Territories, Nunavut, and northern Quebec. Little rain or snow falls there—only 6 to 10 inches (15 to 25 cm) per year—and winds can reach 60 miles per hour (97 kph). The only plants that can survive are wildflowers that grow quickly and make the most of the sunlight during the short summers.

In the summer and fall months, plants in the tundra bloom. This brings huge splashes of color to the tundra.

Cool Living

Since very few producers grow in tundra, there is little food for animals to eat. Animals in tundra ecosystems must be **adapted** to live in the conditions there. Herbivores, such as caribou, use their antlers to dig under snow to find lichens and grasses. Animals also travel hundreds of miles (kilometers) to find food. **Predators**, such as Arctic wolves, travel huge distances to follow their **prey**. The Canadian tundra, like other tundra biomes, has little biodiversity. Only a few plants and animal species can survive there. However, these species need each other to keep the food web in balance.

This map shows where Arctic wolves can be found around the world.

Eco Up Close

The Arctic wolf, also known as the snow wolf, lives in the Canadian Arctic, Alaska, and parts of Greenland. Arctic wolves are **apex predators**. They hunt in packs to catch caribou or musk oxen. The wolves' thick fur protects them from the cold, and they can survive without food for weeks. Wolves and other predators keep the herbivore **populations** low. This keeps herbivores from eating too many producers. Without producers, the food web would collapse.

Arctic wolf

Arctic Archipelago

North of Canada's **mainland**, the Arctic **Archipelago** reaches into the Arctic Ocean. It is made up of 36,563 islands that stretch across the Arctic Ocean, 1,200 miles (1,931 km) north to south and 1,500 miles (2,414 km) east to west. The islands cover an area twice the size of Texas, going as far north as within 500 miles (805 km) of the North Pole! Ice blocks many of the sea channels between the islands of the archipelago. The tundra is much like Canada's northern mainland, but ocean animals such as seals can come ashore and are prey for polar bears.

The flat areas in this picture are where seawater has frozen. Animals travel from one island to the next across the frozen seawater.

All-Day Sun, All-Day Night

Most of the archipelago has polar days and polar nights. Polar days in the middle of the summer are when it can be light for 24 hours a day. Light never appears during polar nights in the winter. Plants have only the short summer months to grow during the long polar days.

Bursting with Life

Arctic wildflowers use summer sunlight to grow. Insects that have been **hibernating** over the winter come out to feed. They **pollinate** flowers. Birds **migrate** to the Arctic to eat insects, while herbivores eat the flowers. Wolves and polar bears eat the herbivores, as well as sea animals that come onto land. Carnivores also **scavenge** dead whales and narwhals.

Eco Focus

The ice creates paths between the archipelago islands for animals such as caribou or polar bears. It also keeps ships from passing through the channels. **Climate change** is causing **sea ice** to melt. What effect will this have on the animals that live on the islands? Explain your thinking.

Eco Up Close

Arctic wildflowers grow close to the ground to avoid high winds. These plants grow well in the rocky soil because it shelters their flowers and seeds. The plants provide food for insects and birds, which in turn help the plants. Insects pollinate the flowers. Birds eat the seeds of plants and spread them in their waste. This helps more plants grow.

Arctic
wildflower

Alaska

The tundra of North America stretches west from Canada into Alaska, then south along the Alaskan coast of the Bering Sea. There, as in northern Canada, lichens and wildflowers are eaten by herbivores, such as moose and caribou. The herbivores become food for predators. The Aleutian Islands, off the coast of Alaska, stretch out into the Pacific Ocean. There, some ocean animals such as sea otters add to the tundra ecosystem.

Surviving Winter

In all tundra ecosystems, animals adapt in many ways to survive the cold winters. Animals that live in tundra all year long have bodies that hold on to heat during the winter. Long ears and tails lose heat quickly so these are shorter on Arctic foxes and hares than those that live farther south. Extra fat helps hold in heat. Other animals, such as the Arctic ground squirrel and the grizzly bear, hibernate to survive the winter.

Traveling South

Another way to survive the tundra ecosystem during the winter is to leave it. Many of the birds found in Alaska's tundra during the summer migrate south during the winter. Snow geese arrive in the tundra in August and September. They feed on sedge plants that bloom for a short period around their arrival. As winter arrives, the geese fly south to Mexico. Tundra swans fly migrate during the winter to live along the coast between Maryland and South Carolina.

There are more than 2,000 different types of plants and producers in Alaska's tundra. They provide food for the herbivores in the food chain.

12

Arctic tern

Eco Up Close

The Arctic tern is the greatest migrator of the Arctic tundra. This bird nests in the Arctic during the summer there, then travels to Antarctica during its summer to feed. It migrates more than 25,000 miles (40,234 km) each year, and so sees more daylight than any other animal on Earth. It also means that the Arctic tern is a regular part of both the Arctic and Antarctic tundra ecosystems.

Eco Focus

Migratory birds time their arrival in the tundra to match the blooming of wildflowers. However, global climate change is causing the growing season to start earlier. How could earlier-blooming plants affect the lives of migratory animals? Explain your thinking.

Siberia

Russia's tundra is found north of the tree line in the vast Siberian plain. Siberian tundra is very cold and dry. It is also home to migrating birds and mammals that eat the wildflowers and grasses that can grow in the tundra's short summers.

The Frozen Earth

All tundra has **permafrost**. This is tundra soil. It is usually made of gravel or sand, and is held together by frozen water, which makes it hard as rock. Tundra soil has two layers. The layer on top freezes in winter and thaws in summer, which is when plants grow in it. The lower layer stays frozen throughout the year.

Plant roots cannot grow deep in permafrost, because the freezing and thawing of the soil breaks the roots. The cold permafrost also slows down the work of decomposers. It takes longer for dead plants and animals to be broken down into nutrients. However, without permafrost, there would be no tundra. The frozen lower layer of permafrost keeps water from draining away, which keeps soil wet in the summer. Otherwise, the tundra would be desert.

Tough Living

In the tough tundra climate, plants must stay low to the ground to avoid wind. They make the most of the warm summers, like the animals that eat them.

Permafrost does not easily drain water. When the top layer of permafrost thaws in the summer, the melted ice becomes water that sits on top of the still-frozen layer of permafrost below. This creates wetlands, or bogs, that plants and birds use.

Eco Up Close

During the tundra summers, the landscape changes to colorful fields of grasses and flowers. For animals hiding from predators such as foxes and wolves, this changed landscape makes it difficult to blend in. However, some animals, like the ermine and the Arctic hare, change their coats in the summer and winter. As winter fades into summer, these animals shed their white winter coats and grow brown summer coats. This helps them blend into the fields, **camouflaging** them from predators.

ermine

Scandinavia and Svalbard

The countries of Scandinavia are called Nordic because they are so far north. However, most of Scandinavia is too warm to have tundra. The Gulf Stream in the Atlantic Ocean carries warm water from the Caribbean Sea, which warms the area. Only Finland's Kola Peninsula, in the far north, has tundra. Tundra is also found in the Arctic Ocean islands north of Scandinavia, such as Norway's Svalbard. This area has polar days and nights. The average summer temperature is just 42.8 degrees Fahrenheit (6 °C).

A Summer Feast

In Svalbard, the cold Arctic air meets warmer, moist air that is carried up from the south. In the summer, this makes rain. As a result, 164 species of grasses and flowers grow here during the summer. They provide food for almost 30 species of migratory birds. The plants also feed the Svalbard reindeer. The birds and reindeer, in turn, provide food for predators such as the Arctic fox and the polar bear. The parts of the Svalbard ecosystem are interdependent.

Eco Focus

The tundra is a fine balance. It is too cold for trees to grow there, but not so cold that wildflowers cannot bloom. It is not so dry that nothing grows, and not so wet that snow covers the ground all year. What might happen to tundra ecosystems if the climate there changes? Explain your thinking.

Svalbard is one of the most northern landmasses in the world. More than 60 percent of it is permanently covered in ice. The rest, pictured here, is tundra.

Eco Up Close

Reindeer, also called caribou, are some of the most common herbivores in Arctic tundra. Like cows, they are **ruminants**. This means that their stomach has four parts to break down grasses. Unlike many animals, reindeer can also eat lichens. They use their antlers to dig into the snow for their food, and their long snouts help them reach deep to take a good bite. The reindeer's clearing of the snow makes it easier for smaller predators to see and hunt smaller mammals. As herbivores, reindeer provide a food chain bridge between plants and carnivores, changing the energy of plants into something carnivores can eat. Without reindeer or other herbivores, many carnivores would starve.

reindeer

Alpine Tundra

The higher above sea level an area is, the colder the temperatures. This is because air rising from sea level gets colder by 11.5 degrees Fahrenheit (6.4 °C) for every 1,000 feet (305 m) it rises. At a very high point above sea level, temperatures become too cold for trees to grow there. The air is dry and windy. Such areas are called **alpine tundra**.

The High Ground

The ecosystems found in alpine tundra are smaller than those of other tundra areas. However, alpine tundra is found wherever the ground rises high above sea level, from Mount Kilimanjaro in Africa to the Himalayas in Asia. As in all tundra ecosystems, plants stay short to avoid the wind, or have dark leaves or red flowers. This is because darker colors **absorb**, or take in, more of the sun's energy. Animals such as hares and mountain goats eat the plants. They are eaten in turn by predators, such as wolves and mountain lions.

Different Tundra, Different Animals

The alpine tundra ecosystems are smaller than other tundra biomes, so fewer and different types of animals are found there. Animals have to adjust to the steep mountain slopes. Large predators found in Arctic tundra, such as polar bears, could not run around the mountains of alpine tundra. However, smaller animals, such as marmots or chinchillas, can climb the cliffs and eat the food, so they survive.

With its jagged, rocky ledges, mountain tundra is a tough place for animals to live.

Eco Up Close

The mountain goat has adapted perfectly to the alpine tundra environment. Like musk oxen and polar bears, it has a thick coat to keep it warm. However, unlike these larger creatures, it can climb steep slopes and stand on narrow ledges. The rough pads under its feet give the goat the grip of a climbing shoe. This helps it survive on the dangerous mountain cliffs.

mountain goat

The Antipodes Subantarctic

The world's smallest area of tundra is found on five island groups south and east of New Zealand. The Bounty Islands, the Auckland Islands, the Antipodes Islands, the Campbell Islands, and Macquarie Island form an area called the Antipodes Subantarctic. The islands have long, dark winters. The wind speed in the Antipodes Subantarctic averages around 25 miles per hour (40 kph).

Wildflowers called megaherbs are found on the Campbell Islands.

Far, Far Away

The islands have the algae, lichens, grasses, **mosses**, and **cushion plants** found in other tundra biomes. However, because they are far from any other land, the Antipodes Islands have different animals and plants from other tundra, including some found nowhere else. They have their own species of butterfly and parakeet, the southernmost tree ferns, and some orchids. They are also home to migrating albatross and penguins. However, no **native** land mammals, **amphibians**, or **reptiles** live there.

Island Invaders

By visiting the islands, people have disturbed the ecosystems. Cats and rats carried on ships have been brought to the islands. These **invasive species** preyed on the islands' natural animals, eating birds' eggs and driving species to **extinction**. New Zealand and Australia's governments have worked hard to remove the cats and rats to protect the ecosystems.

Eco Focus

Why would a species introduced to a new ecosystem be dangerous? What are some of the ways you could control an invasive species if it were introduced to an ecosystem near you? Would introducing predators of the invasive species help, or make things worse? Explain your thinking.

Eco Up Close

The Royal Penguin is an example of a bird species that depends on the islands of the Antipodes Subantarctic. The birds live and feed in waters along the coasts of the Antarctic. However, when it is time for them to breed, they all gather on Macquarie Island. Without the protection of the island, the species would have no **nesting site** and would become extinct.

Royal Penguin

Greenland

East of Canada's Arctic Archipelago is Greenland. Greenland is the world's largest island. It stretches from 500 miles (805 km) south of the Arctic Circle to 500 miles (805 km) south of the North Pole. The island has polar days and polar nights. Two-thirds of the island is covered by an ice sheet that measures up to 1.86 miles (3 km) thick. Greenland's tundra is found on each of the island's coastlines, except the southern one.

A Growing Land

Greenland's tundra is growing as its ice sheet melts due to warming temperatures caused by global climate change. In the past ten years, a number of new islands have appeared off Greenland's east coast as the ice sheet has melted.

Dwarf shrubs, wildflowers, and lichens grow in Greenland's tundra during the summer. They feed musk oxen, caribou, ermines, and Arctic hares. These in turn feed predators, such as Arctic wolves and polar bears. Seals, whales, and narwhals, add to the ecosystem. More than 235 species of birds have been seen in Greenland. Most migrate there and stay just for the summer.

Although the climate of Greenland is very tough, animals such as the Arctic hare have been able to adapt to life there.

Eco Up Close

The musk ox is a large herbivore that lives in Greenland and the Canadian Arctic. Its thick, woolly coat protects it from the cold. The musk ox used to travel across the tundra of Europe, Asia, and Alaska. However, it became extinct in Europe and Asia thousands of years ago because of climate change. The musk ox disappeared from Alaska in the twentieth century because of overhunting by people. This left caribou as the only large herbivore of the Alaskan tundra ecosystem. People are now trying to **reintroduce** the musk ox into the Alaskan tundra.

musk ox

Antarctica

Antarctica is the **continent** with the most extreme living conditions. Located around the South Pole, it is the coldest, driest, and windiest place on Earth. Temperatures can be as low as –128 degrees Fahrenheit (–89 °C). Antarctica is a cold desert. Fewer than 8 inches (200 mm) of rain falls there each year. Giant ice sheets cover 99 percent of Antarctica—the rest is tundra.

Penguins swim through water as easily as most other birds fly through the air! However, they still need to raise their chicks on land.

Deep Freeze

Only a handful of flowering plants, mosses, and lichens grow on Antarctic tundra. Antarctica has just one species of insect— a tiny midge called *Belgica antarctica*. For the animals that do survive on Antarctica, that is not a lot to eat!

Most life in Antarctica is found on its coasts, where the waters and ice of the Southern Ocean meet the land. There, penguins nest and raise their young, before walking for miles (kilometers) to the ocean to catch fish. Antarctica's large predators are leopard seals and whales, which are both marine animals. They feed on penguins that leave the safety of the land to hunt fish in the ocean.

Very Few People

Antarctica is almost untouched by humans. Other than scientists living in research stations, no humans live in Antarctica. They must bring all of their food and supplies with them.

Eco Focus

The scientists in research stations in Antarctica send their garbage back to their home countries on airplanes and ships. Why is the garbage not dumped in Antarctica? What would be the effect on ecosystems if it were? Explain your thinking.

extremophile

Eco Up Close

Extremophiles are organisms that have adapted to survive in difficult conditions, such as high pressure, high temperature, or extreme cold. One example is tiny organisms called **microbes** that have been found in Antarctica's ice. They may even live in a lake miles (kilometers) beneath the surface of Antarctica that has been buried under ice for millions of years! Scientists now believe that microbes may be able to survive in extreme parts of space. They also may be living under the ice of Europa, one of Jupiter's moons.

People and the Tundra

Many indigenous people live in the Arctic tundra. Although these people were among the first to arrive in the tundra, unlike the native species of tundra, they were joining an ecosystem that was already balanced.

Living in Balance

The indigenous people of the Arctic moved into the tundra ecosystem. They took up a place in the food chain that, until other groups of people arrived, was held only by wolves and polar bears. These people began to use tools to hunt animals.

Despite entering the ecosystem, the indigenous peoples of the Arctic lived in balance with it. They hunted only what they needed to survive. They used all parts of the animals they caught. Bones and ivory were made into tools, and skins were used to make clothing.

Changing Everything

European settlers came to the Arctic thousands of years after the indigenous people moved there. They hunted so many animals that the ecosystems were damaged. The musk ox became extinct in Alaska. Wolf and polar bear populations became smaller. Today, countries such as Canada, the United States, and Russia want to drill for oil and natural gas in the Arctic. This will cause even more damage to the ecosystems there.

Eco Up Close

The mammoth is extinct. It once traveled across the plains of Asia and North America. The mammoth lived during the Ice Age, and grew a thick, hairy coat to keep warm. As Earth grew warmer, the mammoth struggled to survive. People who lived during the Ice Age also hunted mammoths and may have hunted them to extinction.

mammoth

Hunting is still important to indigenous people of the Arctic. They hunt animals for food, and to make clothing and tools.

Saving the Tundra

Tundra is a very important part of the world's ecosystems. Losing tundra could mean losing wolves and many migratory birds. This would have an effect on other ecosystems throughout the world. The tundra also captures millions of tons of **greenhouse gases** in permafrost. This keeps the gases out of Earth's atmosphere, and so helps slow down climate change. However, tundra is under threat. The first step to saving tundra and saving the world starts with us.

What Can You Do?

Campaign. Write to politicians about the need to protect tundra.

Help stop pollution and save energy. Walk, bicycle, and use public transportation rather than a car. Switch off lights when they are not being used. By saving energy, we reduce pollution in the Arctic by reducing the need to find more oil and gas in Earth's precious tundras.

Activity:

Create Permafrost!

Find out for yourself the effect of temperature change on permafrost.

You Will Need:

- Plastic bowl
- Water
- Soil (a mixture of garden dirt, gravel, and moss)
- Paper cup
- Pencil

Instructions

1. Fill the plastic bowl with equal parts of water and soil.
2. Mix the parts well and put the mixture in the freezer overnight.
3. The next day, take the mixture out of the freezer. Has it frozen solid? What do you observe?
4. Place the cup on top of the soil to represent a house. Drill a pencil into the soil, to represent a tree.
5. Leave the "permafrost" to thaw. Observe the changes as it melts.

The Challenge

Once your experiment is complete, present it to others and discuss the following questions:

- What happens if you change the soil mixture so there is more gravel, or more dirt?

- Is there a way you can change the cup or the box so it is not affected by the melting permafrost? Test your ideas.

- Research ways you could keep permafrost cold (some ideas can be found at the website **www.cchrc.org/permafrost**).

"permafrost"

Glossary

Please note: Some bold-faced words are defined in the text

abiotic factors Nonliving parts of an ecosystem, such as water and soil

absorb To take in something

adapted Changed over long periods of time or many generations to better suit an environment

algae A group of organisms that have chlorophyll and can make their own food, but are not plants

amphibians Animals, such as frogs and salamanders, that begin life in water, then live on land as adults

apex predators Animals at the top of the food chain, which have few, if any, predators of their own

archipelago A large group or chain of islands

bacteria Living organisms made up of only one cell

biodiversity The variety of plant and animal life in an ecosystem or other area on Earth

biotic factors Living parts of an ecosystem, such as plants and animals

camouflaging Blending in with surroundings

chlorophyll A green substance in plants that changes sunlight and carbon dioxide into energy, which is stored as sugar and used by the plant for food

climate The usual weather in a specific area

climate change A process in which the environment changes to become warmer, colder, drier, or wetter than normal. This can occur naturally, or it can be caused by human activity

continent A landmass, or large area of land, such as North America, Asia, or Australia

cushion plants Low-growing, mat-forming plants that are found in tundras

ecosystem A group of living and nonliving things that live and interact in an area

energy The power that nutrients from food provide to the body

extinction The dying out of a species

food chain A chain of organisms in which each member uses the member below as food

food web The interlinked food chains in an ecosystem

fungi A kind of organism that absorbs food

greenhouse gases Additional gases in the air, such as carbon dioxide or methane, which trap the sun's heat in the atmosphere and keep it from being reflected out into space

hibernating Going into a deep sleep or a long period of inactivity to survive periods of difficult living conditions

indigenous people People who have settled in an area before the arrival of others

interdependent Relying on each other for survival

interrelationships The relationships between many different organisms and their environment

invasive species Animals or plants that have been introduced into an ecosystem where they did not originally live

mainland The large area of land that may have small islands nearby

mammals Warm-blooded animals that have lungs, a backbone, and hair or fur, and drink milk from their mother's body

microbes One-celled organisms, such as bacteria, that feed off other organisms

migrate To travel to another area for food or to reproduce

mosses Small plants that do not have flowers or roots. Mosses grow on damp ground

native Originating from a specific location

nesting site A place where a bird species lays its eggs

nutrients Substances that allow organisms to thrive and grow

organisms Living things

photosynthesis The process in which plants use sunlight to change carbon dioxide and water into food and oxygen

plains Large areas of flat or rolling land

pollinate To transfer pollen grains to the part of a plant that can reproduce

populations The total numbers of species in an area

predators Animals that hunt other animals for food

prey An animal that is hunted by another animal for food

reintroduce To put an organism back into an ecosystem it once lived in

reptiles Animals, like lizards and snakes, that have scales and that rely on the surrounding temperature to warm or cool their bodies

scavenge To feed on the dead remains of other animals

sea ice Frozen water that floats on the surface of polar oceans in huge sheets

species A group of animals or plants that are similar and can produce young

symbiotic relationship A relationship between two different species that can be either helpful or harmful

Learning More

Find out more about Earth's precious tundra ecosystems.

Books

Gazlay, Suzy. *Re-Greening the Environment: Careers in Clean-up, Remediation, and Renewal.* New York, NY: Crabtree Publishing Company, 2011.

Gray, Susan Heinrichs. *Ecology: The Study of Ecosystems.* New York, NY: Scholastic, 2012.

Johnson, Rebecca L. *A Walk in the Tundra* (Biomes of North America). Minneapolis, MN: Carolrhoda, 2001.

Miller, Debbie S. *Survival at 40 Below.* New York, NY: Walker Childrens, 2010.

Slade, Suzanne. *What If There Were No Lemmings?* Mankato, MN: Picture Window, 2010.

Websites

To learn about the Alaska tundra ecosystem, its plants and animals, and how people are affecting it, visit:
www.adfg.alaska.gov/index.cfm?adfg=tundra.main

This site provides an easy-to-understand overview of the various ecosystems of Alaska, including tundra:
www.alaskakids.org/index.cfm/know-alaska/Alaska-Geography/Tundra

Canada's Arctic Tundra explains the plants and animals found in Canada's tundra:
www.hww.ca/en/where-they-live/canadas-arctic-tundra.html

World Wildlife Federation Wild Finder offers a clickable map providing information the world's biomes:
http://worldwildlife.org/science/wildfinder

Index